Around the World
page 8

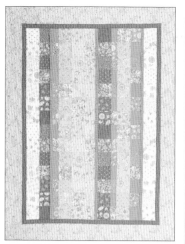

Feminine Frills
page 9

Fresh Air
page 10

ul

from
5"x 5"
Squares

Birds in Flight
pages 50 - 51

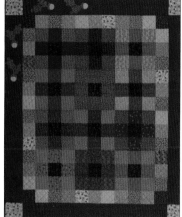

Acorns and Oak Leaves
page 47

By the Sea
pages 48 - 49

Town Square
page 46

Design Tips with 'Charm Squares'

I love quilting with 'Charm' collections of pre-cut 5" x 5" fabric pieces. I want to share a few tips for working with 'Charm Squares'. The colors are always beautiful together and create the hand-made scrappy look that is so popular today.

My first step in designing is to divide the 5" squares into groups of color... Greens, Purples,

Browns, Tans, etc. Next, I estimate the number of squares I will need for the center of the quilt.

Sometimes I need an extra square or two of a color - let's say Dark Brown - so I look for a Tan print with a lot of Brown and move it to the Dark Brown stack.... and the same with other colors.

Enjoy quilting!

Basic Steps

'Charm Squares'
are 5" x 5" fabrics, available
in color-coordinated packs.

'Fat Quarters'
are 22" x 18" fabric pieces,
often available in collections.

Your private stash of assort-
ed fabrics is a wonderful
source for 'scrappy quilts'.

Cut fabric into pieces with
a rotary cutter, quilter's ruler
and cutting mat.

Decadent Victorian

pieced by Donna Perrotta
quilted by Julie Lawson

Deliciously rich, the vibrant colors in this Decadent Victorian quilt enrapture the eye and delight the senses. Create your own Victorian treasure with this wonderful design.

What You'll Need:

SIZE: 52" x 68"

YARDAGE:

We used *Moda* "Decadent Victorian" by April Cornell - we purchased 4 'Charm Packs':
(You'll need a total of 140 squares 5" x 5")

36 Pink	OR	¾ yd
24 Green	OR	½ yd
36 Ivory	OR	¾ yd
30 Purple	OR	⅔ yd
14 Light Ivory	OR	⅓ yd

Inner Border	Purchase ¼ yd Purple
Outer Border & Binding	Purchase 1½ yds Pink
Backing	Purchase 4 yds
Batting	Purchase 60" x 76"

Sewing machine, needle, thread

continued on page 14

Spring Butterflies

pieced by Betty Nowlin
appliqued by Mary Beth Kauffman
quilted by Julie Lawson

Capture the softness of a Spring breeze and the gentle colors that come to life early each year. Beautiful butterflies flutter about the pretty posy garden appliqued on a soft pastel block background.

What You'll Need:

SIZE: 59" x 86"

YARDAGE:
We used *Moda* "Celebrate Spring" by Sandy Gervais
- we purchased 4 'Charm Packs':
(You'll need a total of 160 squares 5" x 5")

4 Coral stripe	OR	⅙ yd
28 Aqua	OR	1 yd
16 Peach	OR	⅓ yd
8 Red	OR	⅓ yd
32 Lime	OR	1 yd
60 Ivory	OR	1⅙ yds
12 Yellow	OR	⅙ yd

Inner Border	Purchase ⅓ yd Aqua
Outer Border & Binding	Purchase 2 yds Green print
Backing	Purchase 4 yds
Batting	Purchase 67" x 94"

Sewing machine, needle, thread

continued on page 16

Around the World

pieced by
Donna Arends Hansen
quilted by
Julie Lawson

For a quilt as playful as the name of its fabric line, Tiddlywinks, this Around the World design is a joy to construct. Simple squares and easy borders make this a fun project, especially for the novice quilter.

Share your love of quilting with a friend or child with colors that bring to mind chocolate, cherries, and ice cream in mint chocolate chip and Superman flavors.

What a delicious, calorie-free way to spend an afternoon!

What You'll Need:

SIZE: 61½" x 70½"
YARDAGE:
We used *Moda* "Tiddlywinks" by Arrin Turnmire
- we purchased 4 'Charm Packs':
(You'll need a total of 143 squares 5" x 5")

20 Turquoise	OR	½ yd
40 Chocolate	OR	¾ yd
27 Pink	OR	½ yd
25 Purple	OR	⅝ yd
31 Green	OR	⅝ yd

Inner Border	Purchase ¼ yd Chocolate
Outer Border & Binding	Purchase 1½ yds Turquoise
Backing	Purchase 3⅝ yds
Batting	Purchase 70" x 79"

Sewing machine, needle, thread

continued on page 22

Feminine Frills

pieced by Betty Nowlin
quilted by Julie Lawson

Perfect for a little girl's room, guest room, or any corner of your home that needs a touch of softness, this romantic pastel quilt will soothe the soul with peaceful prints.

Pleated ruffles add a special finish to this simple design.

What You'll Need:

SIZE: 59½" x 78"

YARDAGE:

We used *Moda* "Little Romance" by April Cornell
we purchased 4 'Charm Packs':
(You'll need a total of 140 squares 5" x 5")

28 White	OR	⅝ yd
28 Lavender	OR	⅝ yd
28 Pink	OR	⅝ yd
28 Green	OR	⅝ yd
28 Light Pink	OR	⅝ yd

Ruffle	Purchase 1 yd Pink
Inner Border	Purchase ⅜ yd Lavender
Outer Border & Binding	Purchase 2 yds Pink Floral
Backing	Purchase 3½ yds
Batting	Purchase 68" x 86"
Sewing machine, needle, thread	

continued on page 24

Fresh Air

pieced by
Donna Perrotta
quilted by
Julie Lawson

Unleash your inner child with playful patterns and a confetti spray of dramatic color.

This eclectic, retro look quilt is sure to exude joy and bring attention.

What You'll Need:

SIZE: 59" x 77"

YARDAGE:
We used *Moda* "Fresh Air" by Chez Moi
- we purchased 4 'Charm Packs':
(You'll need a total of 140 squares 5" x 5")

4 Green	OR	⅙ yd
35 Red	OR	¾ yd
24 Chocolate	OR	½ yd
34 Orange	OR	¾ yd
21 Blue	OR	½ yd
22 Purple	OR	½ yd

Inner Border	Purchase ¼ yd Chocolate
Outer Border & Binding	Purchase 2 yds Rust print
Backing	Purchase 3½ yds
Batting	Purchase 67" x 85"

Sewing machine, needle, thread

continued on page 26

Basic Sewing Instructions

You now have precisely cut pieces. You are well on your way to blocks that fit together perfectly. Accurate sewing is the next important step.

Matching Edges:

1. Carefully line up the edges of your fabric. Many times, if the underside is off a little, your seam will be off by $\frac{1}{8}$". This does not sound like much until you have 8 seams in a block, each off by $\frac{1}{8}$". Now your finished block is a whole inch wrong!

2. Pin the pieces together to prevent them shifting.

Seam Allowance:

I cannot stress enough the importance of accurate $\frac{1}{4}$" seams. All the quilts in this book are measured for $\frac{1}{4}$" seams unless otherwise indicated.

Most sewing machine manufacturers offer a Quarter-inch foot. A Quarter-inch foot is the most worthwhile investment you can make in your quilting.

Pressing:

I want to talk about pressing even before we get to sewing because proper pressing can make the difference between a quilt that wins a ribbon at the quilt show and one that does not.

Press, do NOT iron. What does that mean? Many of us want to move the iron back and forth along the seam. This "ironing" stretches the fabric out of shape and creates errors that accumulate as the quilt is constructed. Believe it or not, there is a correct way to press your seams, and here it is:

1. Do NOT use steam with your iron. If you need a little water, spritz it on.

2. Place your fabric flat on the ironing board without opening the seam. Set a hot iron on the seam and count to 3. Lift the iron and move to the next position along the seam. Repeat until the entire seam is pressed. This sets and sinks the threads into the fabric.

3. Now, carefully lift the top fabric and fold it away from you so the seam is on one side. Usually the seam is pressed toward the darker fabric, but often the direction of the seam is determined by the piecing requirements.

4. Press the seam flat with your fingers. Add a little water or spray starch if it wants to close again. Lift the iron and place it on the seam. Count to 3. Lift the iron again and continue until the seam is pressed. Do NOT use the tip of the iron to push the seam flat. So many people do this and wonder later why their blocks are not fitting together.

5. Most critical of all: For accuracy every seam must be pressed before the next seam is sewn.

Working with 'Crosswise Grain' strips:

Strips cut on the crosswise grain (from selvage to selvage) have problems similar to bias edges and are prone to stretching. To reduce stretching and make your quilt lay flat for quilting, keep these tips in mind.

1. Take care not to stretch the fabric as you sew.

2. Adjust the sewing thread tension and the presser foot pressure if needed.

3. If you detect any puckering as you go, rip out the seam and sew it again. It is much easier to take out a seam now than to do it after the block is finished.

Sewing Bias Edges:

Bias edges wiggle and stretch out of shape very easily. They are not recommended for beginners, but even a novice can accomplish bias edges if these techniques are employed.

1. Stabilize the bias edge with one of these methods:

  a) Press with spray starch.

  b) Press freezer paper or removable iron-on stabilizer to the back of the fabric.

  c) Sew a double row of stay stitches along the bias edge and $\frac{1}{8}$" from the bias edge. This is a favorite technique of garment makers.

2. Pin, pin, pin! I know many of us dislike pinning, but when working with bias edges, pinning makes the difference between intersections that match and those that do not.

Building Better Borders:

Wiggly borders make a quilt very difficult to finish. However, wiggly borders can be avoided with these techniques.

1. Cut the borders on grain. That means cutting your vertical strips parallel to the selvage edge. The horizontal strips are cut on the cross-wise grain.

2. Accurately cut your borders to the exact measure of the quilt.

3. If your borders are pieced from crosswise grain fabrics, press well with spray starch and sew a double row of stay stitches along the outside edge to maintain the original shape and prevent stretching.

4. Pin the border to the quilt, taking care not to stretch the quilt top to make it fit. Pinning reduces slipping and stretching.

Applique Instructions

Basic Turned Edge

1. Trace pattern onto template plastic.

2. Cut out the shape leaving a scant ¼" fabric border all around and clip the curves.

3. Place the template plastic on the wrong side of the fabric. Spray edges with starch.

4. Press the ⅛" border over the edge of the template plastic with the tip of a hot iron. Press firmly.

5. Remove the template, maintaining the folded edge on the back of the fabric.

6. Position the shape on the quilt and Blindstitch in place.

Basic Needle Turn

1. Cut out the shape leaving a ¼" fabric border all around.

2. Baste the shapes to the quilt, keeping the basting stitches away from the edge of the fabric.

3. Begin with all areas that are under other layers and work to the topmost layer.

4. For an area no more than 2" ahead of where you are working, trim to ⅛" and clip the curves.

5. Using the needle, roll the edge under and sew tiny Blindstitches to secure.

Using Fusible Web for Iron-on Applique:

1. Trace the pattern onto *Steam a Seam 2* fusible web.

2. Press the patterns onto the wrong side of the fabric.

3. Cut out patterns exactly on the drawn line.

4. Score the web paper with a pin, then remove the paper.

5. Position the fabric, fusible side down, on the quilt. Press with a hot iron following the fusible web manufacturer's instructions.

6. Stitch around the edge by hand.

Optional: Stabilize the wrong side of the fabric with your favorite stabilizer.

Use a size 80 machine embroidery needle. Fill the bobbin with lightweight basting thread and thread the machine with a machine embroidery thread that complements the color being appliqued.

Set your machine for a Zigzag stitch and adjust the thread tension if needed. Use a scrap to experiment with different stitch widths and lengths until you find the one you like best.

Sew slowly.

Tips for Quality Workmanship

These tips will help reduce stretching and make your quilt lay flat for quilting.

1. If you are cutting yardage, cut on the grain.

2. When sewing crosswise grain strips together, take care not to stretch the strips. If you detect any puckering as you go, rip out the seam and sew it again.

3. Press, Do Not Iron. Press without moving the iron. A back-and-forth ironing motion stretches the fabric.

4. √For smooth quilting, press all seams to one side rather than pressing them open.

5. Reduce the wiggle in your borders with this technique from garment making. First, accurately cut your borders to the exact measure of the quilt top. Then, before sewing the border to the quilt, run a double row of stay stitches along the outside edge to maintain the original shape and prevent stretching. Pin the border to the quilt, taking care not to stretch the quilt top to make it fit. Pinning reduces slipping and stretching.

Rotary Cutting Tips

Rotary Cutter: Friend or Foe

A rotary cutter is a wonderful and useful tool. When not used correctly, the sharp blade can be dangerous.
Follow these safety tips:

1. Never cut toward you.

2. Use a sharp blade. Pressing harder on a dull blade can cause the blade to jump the ruler and injure your fingers.

3. Always disengage the blade before the cutter leaves your hand, even if you intend to pick it up immediately.

Rotary cutters have been caught when lifting fabric, have fallen onto the floor and have cut feet, legs and fingers.

Basic Cutting Instructions

Tips for Accurate Cutting:

Accurate cutting is easy when using a rotary cutter with a sharp blade, a cutting mat, and a transparent ruler. Begin by pressing your fabric and then follow these steps:

1. Folding:

a) Fold the fabric with the selvage edges together. Smooth the fabric flat. If needed, fold again to make your fabric length smaller than the length of the ruler.

b) Align the fold with one of the guide lines on the mat. This is important to avoid getting a kink in your fabric.

2. Cutting:

a) Align the ruler with a guide line on the mat. Press down on the ruler to prevent it shifting or have someone help hold the ruler. Hold the rotary cutter along the edge of the ruler and cut off the selvage edge.

b) Also using the guide line on the mat, cut the ends straight.

c) Cut strips for making the quilt top on 'crosswise grain' (from selvage to selvage) or 'on grain' (parallel to the selvage edge).

If possible, cut strips for borders on grain (parallel to the selvage edge) to prevent wavy edges and make quilting easier.

d) When cutting strips, move the ruler, NOT the fabric.

Basic Layering Instructions

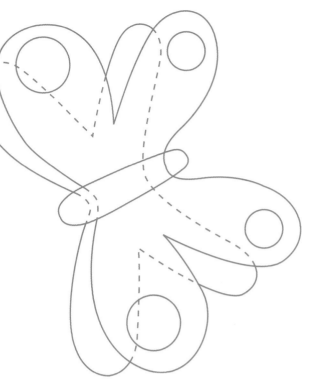

Marking Your Quilt:

If you choose to mark your quilt for hand or machine quilting, it is much easier to do so before layering. Press your quilt before you begin. Here are some handy tips regarding marking.

1. A disappearing pen may vanish before you finish.

2. Use a White pencil on dark fabrics.

3. If using a washable Blue pen, remember that pressing may make the pen permanent.

Pieced Backings:

1. Press the backing fabric before measuring.

2. If possible cut backing fabrics on grain, parallel to the selvage edges.

3. Piece 3 parts rather than 2 whenever possible, sewing 2 side borders to the center. This reduces stress on the pieced seam.

4. The backing and batting should extend at least 2" on each side of the quilt.

Creating a Quilt Sandwich:

1. Press the backing and top to remove all wrinkles.

2. Lay the backing wrong side up on the table.

3. Position the batting over the backing and smooth out all wrinkles.

4. Center the quilt top over the batting leaving a 2" border all around.

5. Pin the layers together with 2" safety pins positioned a handwidth apart. A grapefruit spoon makes inserting the pins easier. Leaving the pins open in the container speeds up the basting on the next quilt.

Basic Quilting Instructions

Hand Quilting:

Many quilters enjoy the serenity of hand quilting. Because the quilt is handled a great deal, it is important to securely baste the sandwich together. Place the quilt in a hoop and don't forget to hide your knots.

Machine Quilting:

All the quilts in this book were machine quilted. Some were quilted on a large, free-arm quilting machine and others were quilted on a sewing machine. If you have never machine quilted before, practice on some scraps first.

Straight Line Machine Quilting Tips:

1. Pin baste the layers securely.

2. Set up your sewing machine with a size 80 quilting needle and a walking foot.

3. Experimenting with the decorative stitches on your machine adds interest to your quilt. You do not have to quilt the entire piece with the same stitch. Variety is the spice of life, so have fun trying out stitches you have never used before as well as your favorite stand-bys.

Free Motion Machine Quilting Tips:

1. Pin baste the layers securely.

2. Set up your sewing machine with a spring needle, a quilting foot, and lower the feed dogs.

photo on page 4

Decadent Victorian

SIZE: 52" x 68"

YARDAGE:
We used *Moda* "Decadent Victorian" by April Cornell
- we purchased 4 'Charm Packs':
(You'll need a total of 140 squares 5" x 5")

36 Pink	OR	¾ yd
24 Green	OR	½ yd
36 Ivory	OR	¾ yd
30 Purple	OR	⅔ yd
14 Light Ivory	OR	⅓ yd

Inner Border	Purchase ¼ yd Purple
Outer Border & Binding	Purchase 1½ yds Pink
Backing	Purchase 4 yds
Batting	Purchase 60" x 76"

Sewing machine, needle, thread

SORTING:
Set aside the following 5" x 5" squares and trim to 4½" x 4½":
    16 Green
    16 Pink
    16 Purple
    28 Ivory
    12 Light Ivory
Set aside the following 5" x 5" squares to make half-square triangles:
    14 Purple
    8 Ivory
    8 Green
    20 Pink
    2 Light Ivory

HALF-SQUARE TRIANGLES:
Match the following squares for the half-square triangles:
    2 pairs of Purple- Ivory
    2 pairs of Green-Ivory
    6 pairs of Pink-Green
    4 pairs of Pink-Ivory
    10 pairs of Pink-Purple
    2 pairs of Purple-Light Ivory

HOW TO MAKE HALF-SQUARE TRIANGLES:
See Half-Square Triangle Diagram.
Place 2 squares with right sides together.
Using a pencil or washable marker, draw 1 diagonal line.
Sew a ¼" seam on each side of the diagonal.
Cut on the diagonal. Press square open.

ASSEMBLY:
Follow the Quilt Assembly Diagram.
Arrange squares in 14 rows, 10 squares per row.
Sew the squares together to form rows. Press.
Sew the rows together. Press.

BORDERS:
Purple Inner Border:
Cut 2 side strips 1½" x 56½".
Cut top and bottom strips 1½" x 42½".
Sew side borders to the quilt. Press.
Sew the top and bottom borders. Press.

Outer Border:
Cut 2 side strips 5½" x 58½".
Cut the top and bottom strips 5½" x 52½".
Sew side borders to the quilt. Press.
Sew the top and bottom borders. Press.

FINISH:
Quilting: See Basic Quilting Instructions on page 13.
Binding: Cut 2½" strips.
        Sew strips together end to end to make 250".
        Follow Binding Instructions on page 42.

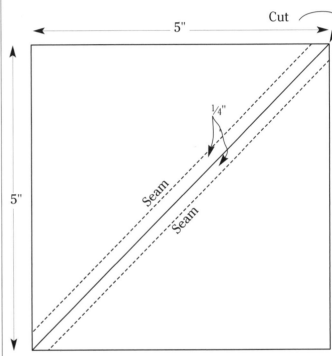

Half-Square Triangle Diagram
1. Place 2 squares right side together.
2. Draw a diagonal line from corner to corner.
3. Stitch ¼" on each side of the line.
4. Cut squares apart on the diagonal line.
5. Open the 2 new squares with 2 colors.
6. Press. Trim off dog-ears.
7. Trim to 4½" x 4½".

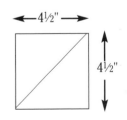

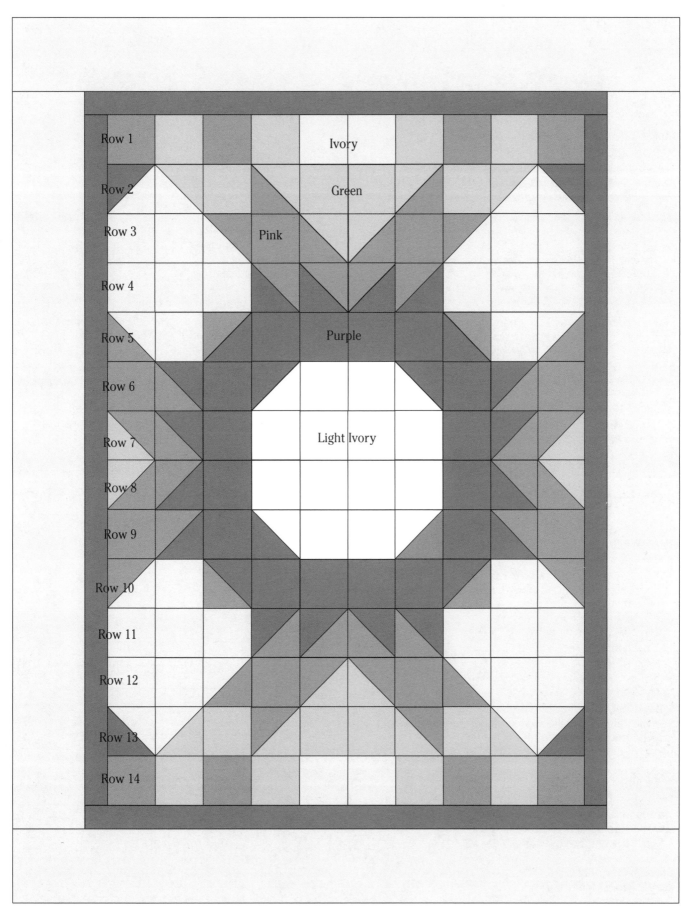

Row 1   Ivory

Row 2   Green

Row 3   Pink

Row 4

Row 5   Purple

Row 6

Row 7   Light Ivory

Row 8

Row 9

Row 10

Row 11

Row 12

Row 13

Row 14

Decadent Victorian
Quilt Assembly Diagram

Spring Butterflies

SIZE: 59" x 86"
YARDAGE:
We used *Moda* "Celebrate Spring" by Sandy Gervais
- we purchased 4 'Charm Packs':
(You'll need a total of 160 squares 5" x 5")

4 Coral stripe	OR	⅙ yd
28 Aqua	OR	1 yd
16 Peach	OR	⅓ yd
8 Red	OR	⅓ yd
32 Lime	OR	1 yd
60 Ivory	OR	1⅙ yds
12 Yellow	OR	⅙ yd

Inner Border	Purchase ⅓ yd Aqua
Outer Border & Binding	Purchase 2 yds Green print
Backing	Purchase 4 yds
Batting	Purchase 67" x 94"

Sewing machine, needle, thread

Applique Fabrics:
¼ yd Aqua
⅛ yd Peach
⅓ yd Red
⅙ yd Lime
⅙ yd Yellow
DMC Green pearl cotton

4-PATCH ASSEMBLY:
Sew the following 4-Patches:
 4   Corner blocks
        Each block uses 2 Red, 1 Lime, 1 Coral stripe
        See the Quilt Assembly Diagram for placement.
 15   Ivory
 7   Aqua
 5   Peach
 7   Lime
 2   Yellow

ASSEMBLY:
Follow the Quilt Assembly Diagram.
Sew the patches into 8 rows, 5 patches per row. Press.
Sew the rows together. Press.

BORDERS:
Aqua Inner Border:
Cut 2 side strips 1½" x 72½".
Cut top and bottom strips 1½" x 47½".
Sew the side borders to the quilt. Press.
Add the top and bottom borders. Press.

Green Outer Border:
Cut 2 side strips 6½" x 74½".
Cut top and bottom strips 6½" x 59½".
Sew the side borders to the quilt. Press.
Add the top and bottom borders. Press.

APPLIQUE:
Cut out the following pieces using patterns:
See patterns on pages 18 - 21.
    3 Red wing #1
    3 Aqua wing #2
    3 Red body #3
    6 Peach large spot #4
    6 Lime small spot #5
    6 Red petal #1
    6 Yellow center #2
    6 Lime center #3
    6 Lime leaf #4
    6 Lime leaf #5

See Applique Instructions on page 11.
Embroider antennae and flower stems with a
    Running stitch and Green pearl cotton.

FINISH:
Quilting: See Basic Quilting Instructions on page 13.
Binding: Cut 2½" strips.
        Sew strips together end to end to make 300".
        Follow Binding Instructions on page 42.

Applique Placement Diagram

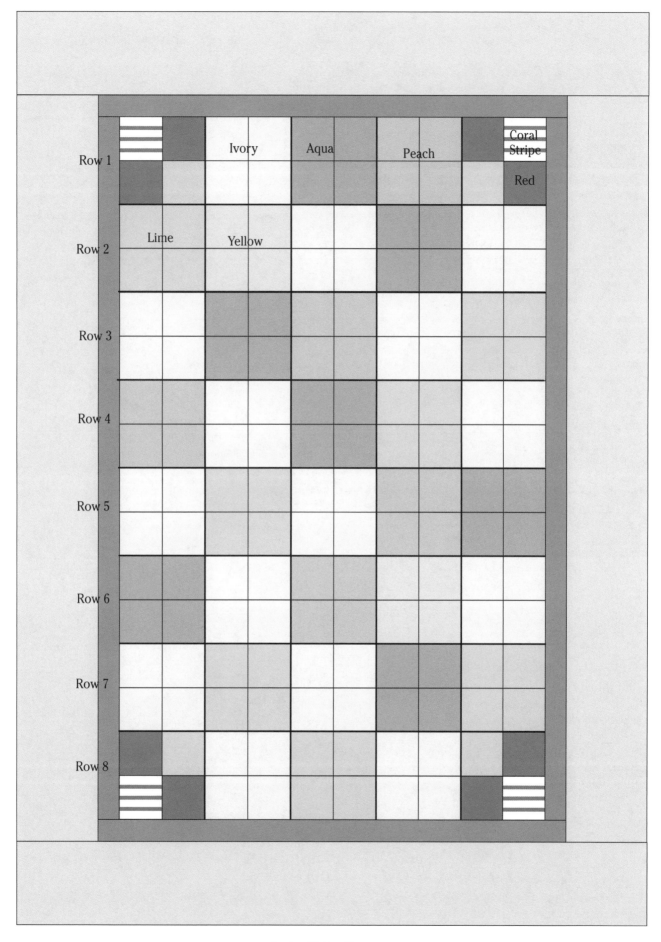

Spring Butterflies
Quilt Assembly Diagram

continued on page 18

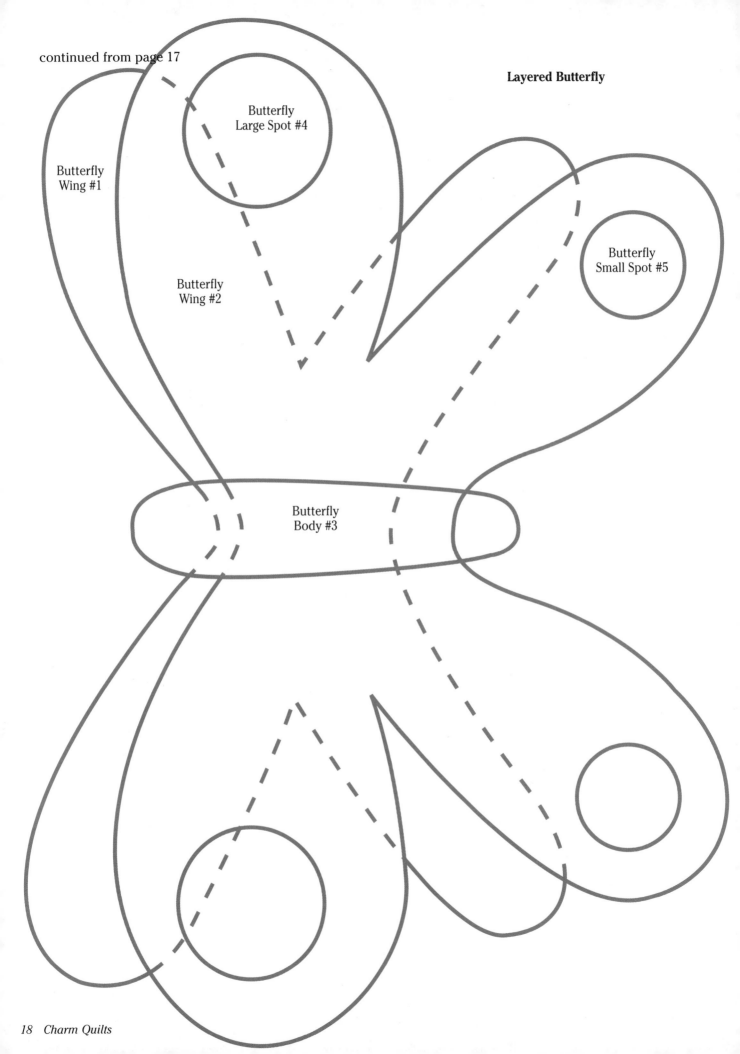

continued from page 17

Layered Butterfly

Butterfly
Large Spot #4

Butterfly
Wing #1

Butterfly
Small Spot #5

Butterfly
Wing #2

Butterfly
Body #3

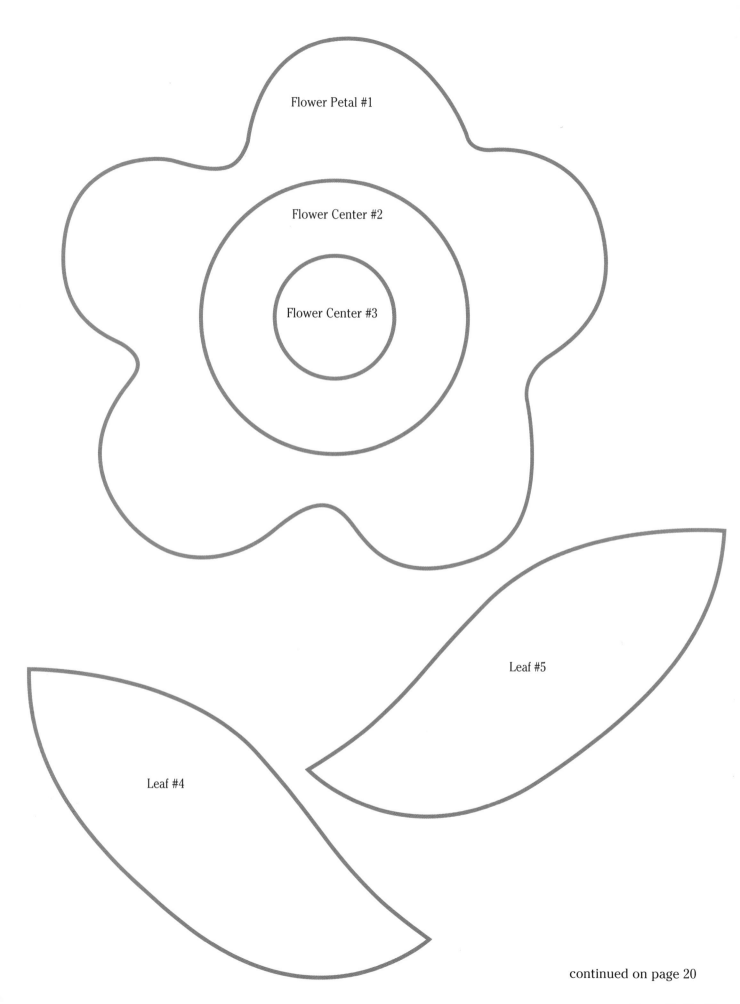

Flower Petal #1

Flower Center #2

Flower Center #3

Leaf #5

Leaf #4

continued on page 20

continued from page 19

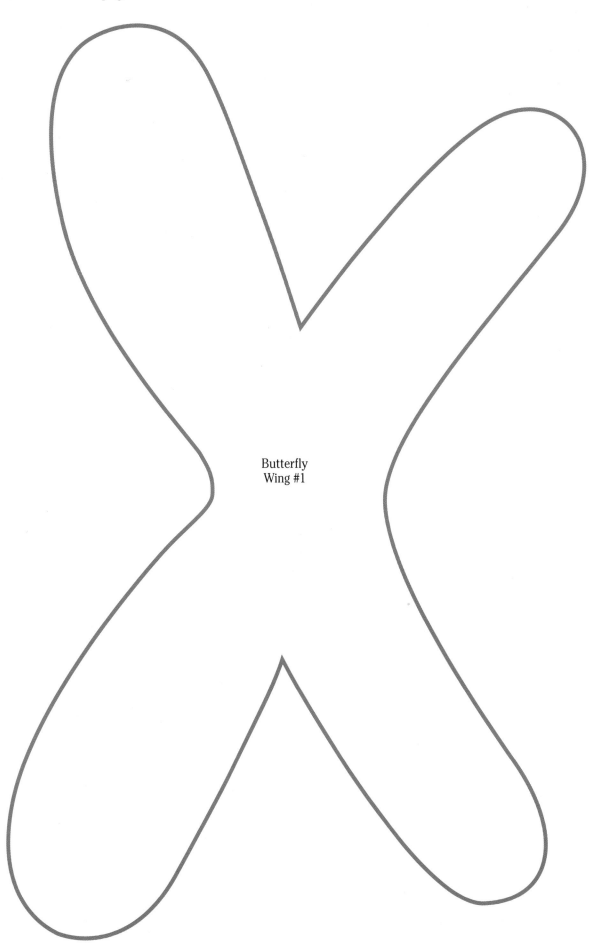

Butterfly
Wing #1

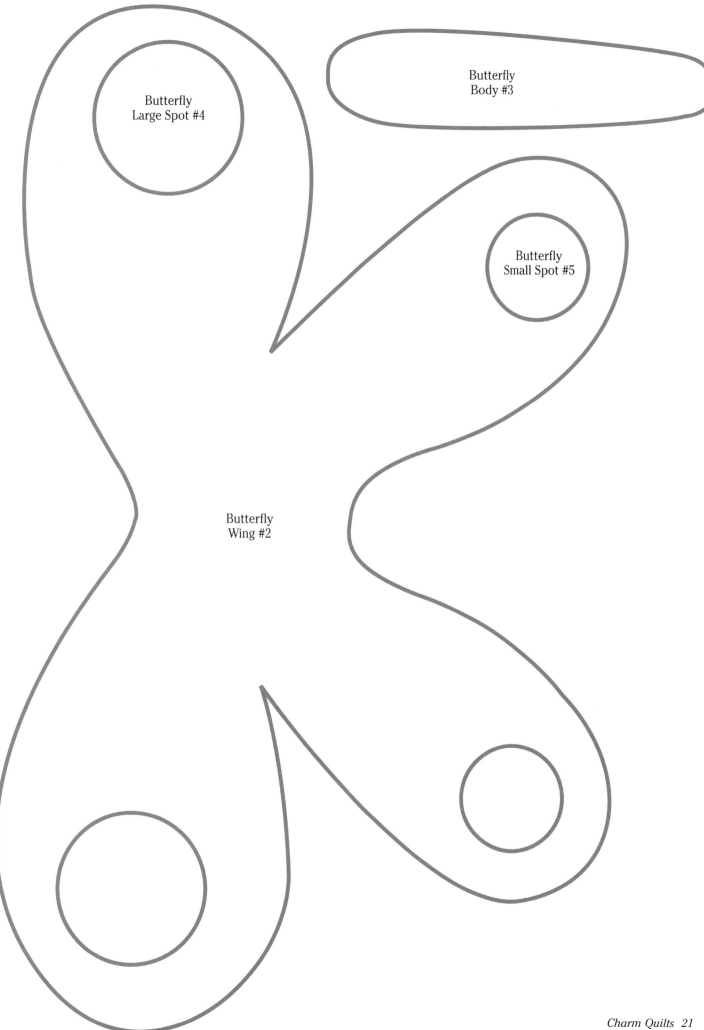

Butterfly
Body #3

Butterfly
Large Spot #4

Butterfly
Small Spot #5

Butterfly
Wing #2

Around the World

SIZE: 61½" x 70½"

YARDAGE:
We used *Moda* "Tiddlywinks" by Arrin Turnmire
- we purchased 4 'Charm Packs'
(You'll need a total of 143 squares 5" x 5")

20 Turquoise	OR	½ yd
40 Chocolate	OR	¾ yd
27 Pink	OR	½ yd
25 Purple	OR	⅝ yd
31 Green	OR	⅝ yd

Inner Border   Purchase ¼ yd Chocolate
Outer Border & Binding   Purchase 1½ yds Turquoise
Backing   Purchase 3⅝ yds
Batting   Purchase 70" x 79"
Sewing machine, needle, thread

Turquoise

Chocolate

Pink

Purple

Green

ASSEMBLY:
Follow the Assembly Diagram.
Arrange squares in 13 rows, 11 squares per row.
Sew squares together to form each row. Press.
Sew the rows together. Press.

BORDERS:
Chocolate Inner Border:
Cut side strips 1½" x 61".
Cut top and bottom strips 1½" x 50".
Sew the top and bottom borders to the quilt. Press.
Sew side borders to the quilt. Press.

Turquoise Outer Border:
Cut side strips 5½" x 61".
Cut top and bottom strips 5½" x 62".
Sew side borders to the quilt. Press.
Sew top and bottom borders to the quilt. Press.

FINISH:
Quilting: See Basic Quilting Instructions on page 13.
Binding: Cut 2½" strips.
             Sew strips together end to end to make 274".
             Follow Binding Instructions on page 42.

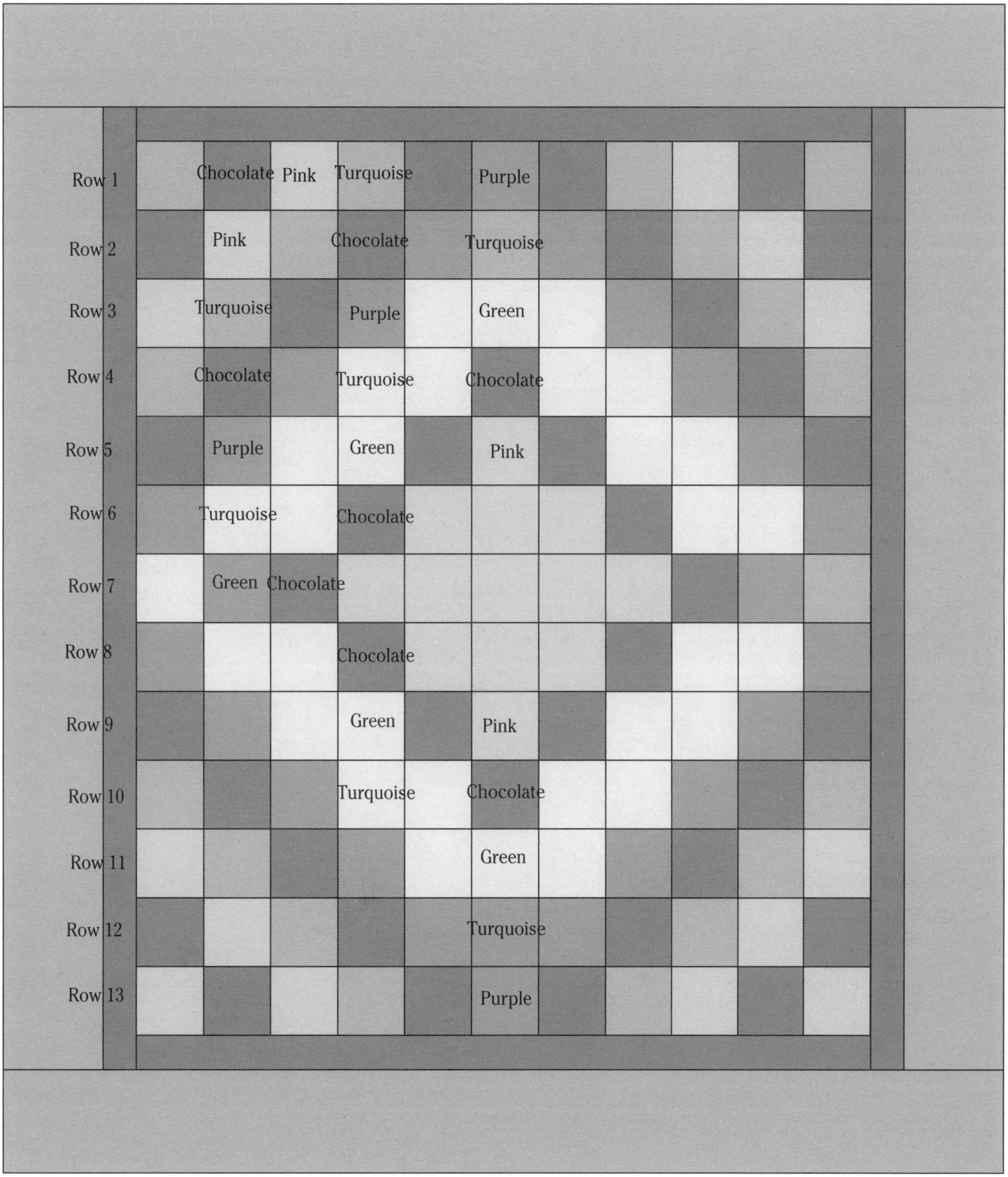

Row 1		Chocolate	Pink	Turquoise		Purple						
Row 2		Pink		Chocolate		Turquoise						
Row 3		Turquoise		Purple		Green						
Row 4		Chocolate		Turquoise		Chocolate						
Row 5		Purple		Green		Pink						
Row 6		Turquoise		Chocolate								
Row 7		Green	Chocolate									
Row 8				Chocolate								
Row 9				Green		Pink						
Row 10				Turquoise		Chocolate						
Row 11						Green						
Row 12						Turquoise						
Row 13						Purple						

Around the World
Quilt Assembly Diagram

photo on page 9

Feminine Frills

SIZE: 59½" x 78"
YARDAGE:
We used *Moda* "Little Romance" by April Cornell
- we purchased 4 'Charm Packs':
(You'll need a total of 140 squares 5" x 5")

28 White	OR	⅝ yd
28 Lavender	OR	⅝ yd
28 Pink	OR	⅝ yd
28 Green	OR	⅝ yd
28 Light Pink	OR	⅝ yd

Ruffle   Purchase 1 yd Pink
Inner Border   Purchase ⅜ yd Lavender
Outer Border & Binding   Purchase 2 yds Pink Floral
Backing   Purchase 3½ yds
Batting   Purchase 68" x 86"
Sewing machine, needle, thread

SEW COLUMNS:
All the blocks in a column are the same color.
You will sew and press 10 column strips with 14 blocks in each column:
    2 White, 2 Lavender, 2 Pink, 2 Green, and 2 Light Pink
Cut 1 of the Pink strips in half lengthwise to make 2 strips 2½" x 63½".

ADD RUFFLE:
Sew a ruffle strip to the right side of the Lavender strip for column 2.
Sew a ruffle strip to the right side of the Light Pink strip for column 6.
Sew a ruffle strip to the right side of the Pink strip for column 10.

ASSEMBLE COLUMNS:
Follow the Assembly Diagram.
Sew the columns together. Press.
Between columns 2 and 3, 6 and 7, 10 and 11, sandwich the raw edge of the ruffle in the seam. Press.

Lavender Inner Border:
Cut 2 side strips 2" x 63½".
Cut top and bottom strips 2" x 48".
Sew side borders to the quilt. Press.
Sew the top and bottom borders to the quilt. Press.

Pink Outer Border:
Cut 2 side strips 6½" x 66½".
Cut top and bottom strips 6½" x 60".
Sew the side borders to the quilt. Press.
Sew top and bottom borders to the quilt. Press.

FINISH:
Quilting: See Basic Quilting Instructions on page 13.
Binding: Cut 2½" strips.
               Sew strips together end to end to make 285".
               Follow Binding Instructions on page 42.

Make the Ruffles

Cut 12 strips 2½" x 43".
See Diagram for Bias Binding for ruffle.

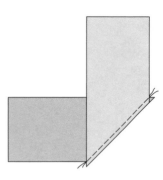

TIP: You must sew the ends together on the bias or the strip will be too thick to feed through the ruffler.

Sew strips end to end to make 3 strips 158" long.

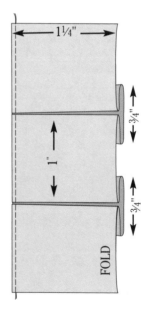

Fold each strip in half lengthwise to make a strip 1¼" x 158".

Set the ruffle foot of your sewing machine for box pleat and sew along the raw edge, leaving ½" tails at each end. Make 3 ruffle strips 63½" long.

TIP: You can pleat this by hand using the Box Pleat Diagram above.

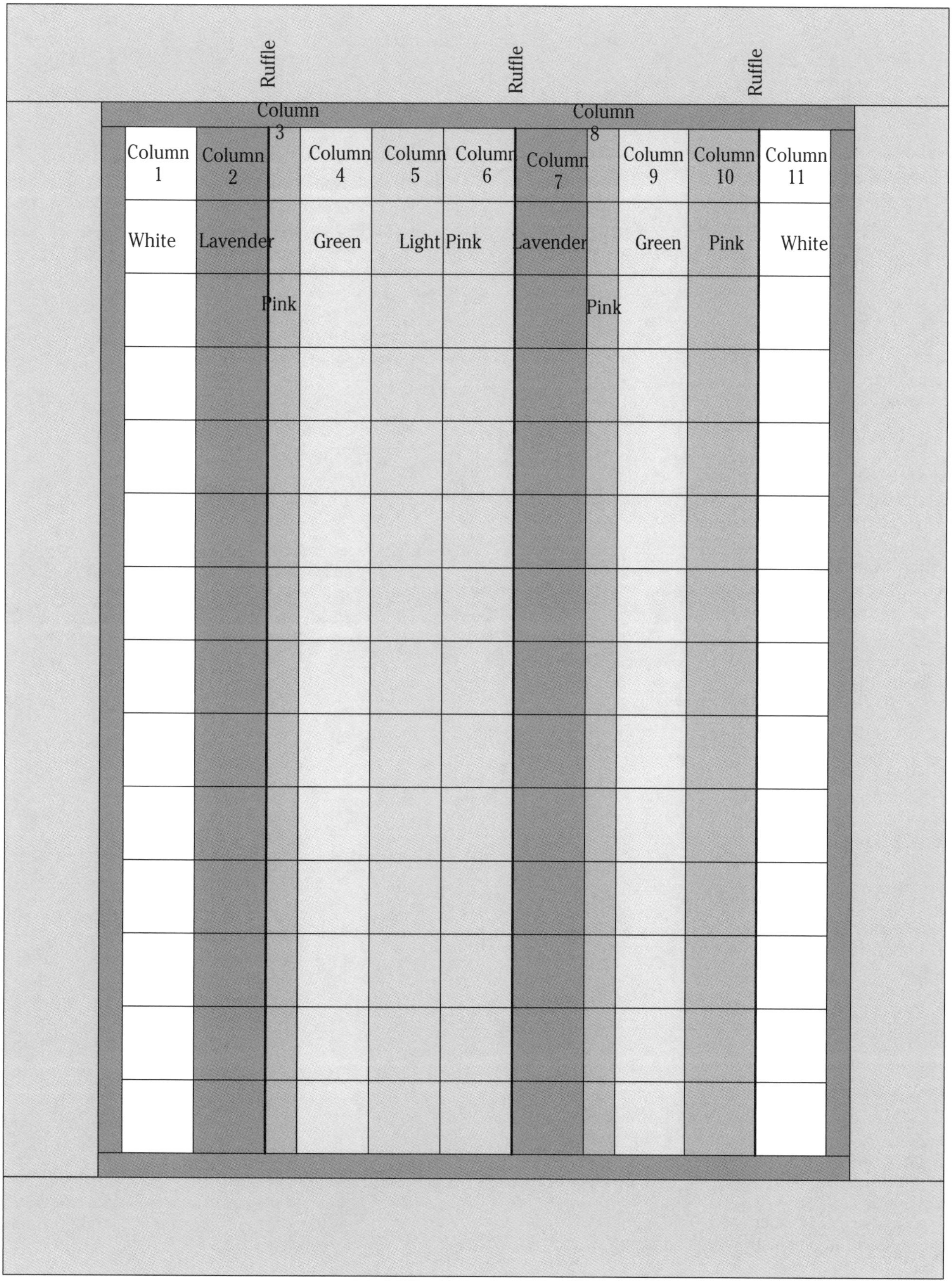

Column 1	Column 2	Column 3	Column 4	Column 5	Column 6	Column 7	Column 8	Column 9	Column 10	Column 11
White	Lavender		Green	Light	Pink	Lavender		Green	Pink	White
		Pink					Pink			

Feminine Frills
Quilt Assembly Diagram

Fresh Air

SIZE: 59" x 77"

YARDAGE:
We used *Moda* "Fresh Air" by Chez Moi
- we purchased 4 'Charm Packs':
(You'll need a total of 140 squares 5" x 5")

4 Green	OR	⅙ yd
35 Red	OR	¾ yd
24 Chocolate	OR	½ yd
34 Orange	OR	¾ yd
21 Blue	OR	½ yd
22 Purple	OR	½ yd

Inner Border	Purchase ¼ yd Chocolate
Outer Border & Binding	Purchase 2 yds Rust print
Backing	Purchase 3½ yds
Batting	Purchase 67" x 85"

Sewing machine, needle, thread

4-PATCH ASSEMBLY:
Sew the following 4-Patches:
- 4   Blue
- 4   Chocolate
- 4   Orange
- 4   Purple
- 4   Red

ASSEMBLY:
Follow the Assembly Diagram.
    Sew 5 rows with 4 blocks in each row. Press.
    Sew the rows together. Press.

BORDERS:
Pieced Border #1:
Follow the Assembly Diagram for color placement.
    Sew 2 side strips using 10 squares each. Press.
    Sew side borders to the quilt. Press.

    Sew 4 strips using 10 squares each for the top and
        bottom borders. Press.
    Sew 2 strips to the top and 2 strips to the bottom.
        Press.

Chocolate Inner Border:
    Cut 2 side strips 1½" x 63½".
    Cut top and bottom strips 1½" x 47½".

    Sew side borders to the quilt. Press.
    Sew the top and bottom borders. Press.

Rust Outer Border:
    Cut 2 side strips 6½" x 65½".
    Cut top and bottom strips 6½" x 59½".

    Sew side borders to the quilt. Press.
    Sew the top and bottom borders. Press.

FINISH:
Quilting: See Basic Quilting Instructions on page 13.
Binding: Cut 2½" strips.
        Sew strips together end to end to make 282".
        Follow Binding Instructions on page 42.

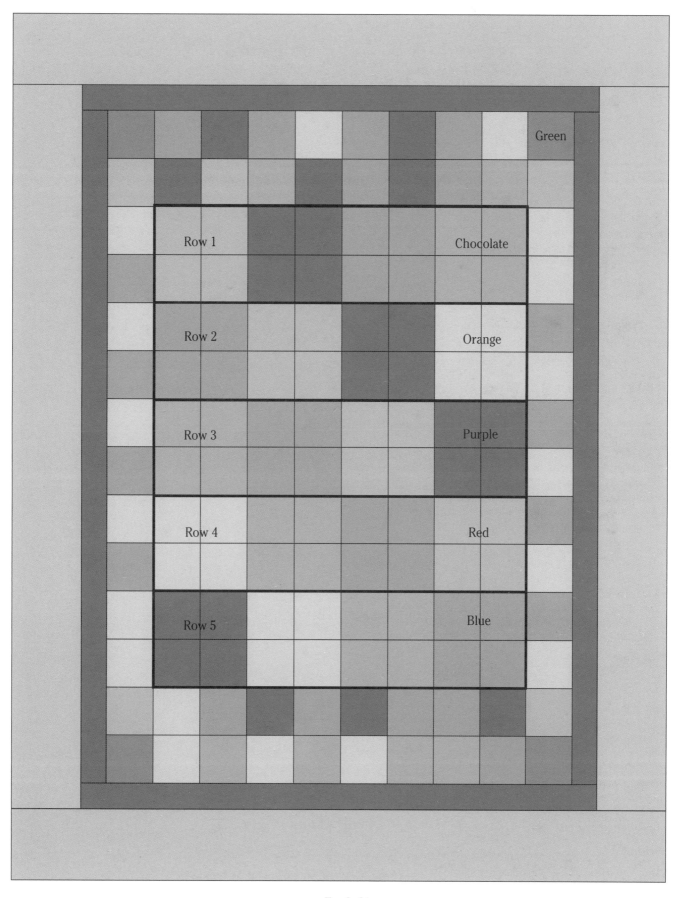

Green

Row 1   Chocolate

Row 2   Orange

Row 3   Purple

Row 4   Red

Row 5   Blue

Fresh Air
Quilt Assembly Diagram

photo on page 43

Retro Blossoms

SIZE: 57" x 70½"

YARDAGE:
We used *Moda* "Blossom" by Urban Chiks
- we purchased 4 'Charm Packs':
(You'll need a total of 130 squares 5" x 5")

10 Gold	OR	⅓ yd
30 Coral	OR	⅝ yd
30 Lime	OR	⅝ yd
34 Chocolate	OR	¾ yd
26 White	OR	⅝ yd

Inner Border	Purchase ¼ yd Chocolate
Outer Border & Binding	Purchase 1½ yds Floral
Backing	Purchase 3¼ yds
Batting	Purchase 65" x 79"

Sewing machine, needle, thread

ASSEMBLY:
Follow the Assembly Diagram.
Arrange squares in 13 rows, 10 squares per row.
> Sew squares together to form each row. Press.
> Sew rows together. Press.

BORDERS:
Chocolate Inner Border:
> Cut 2 side strips 1½" x 59".
> Cut top and bottom strips 1½" x 47½".

> Sew side borders to the quilt. Press.
> Sew top and bottom borders. Press.

Floral Outer Border:
> Cut 2 side strips 5½" x 61".
> Cut top and bottom strips 5½" x 57½".

> Sew side borders to the quilt. Press.
> Sew top and bottom borders. Press.

FINISH:
Quilting: See Basic Quilting Instructions on page 13.
Binding: Cut 2½" strips.
> Sew strips together end to end to make 263".
> Follow Binding Instructions on page 42.

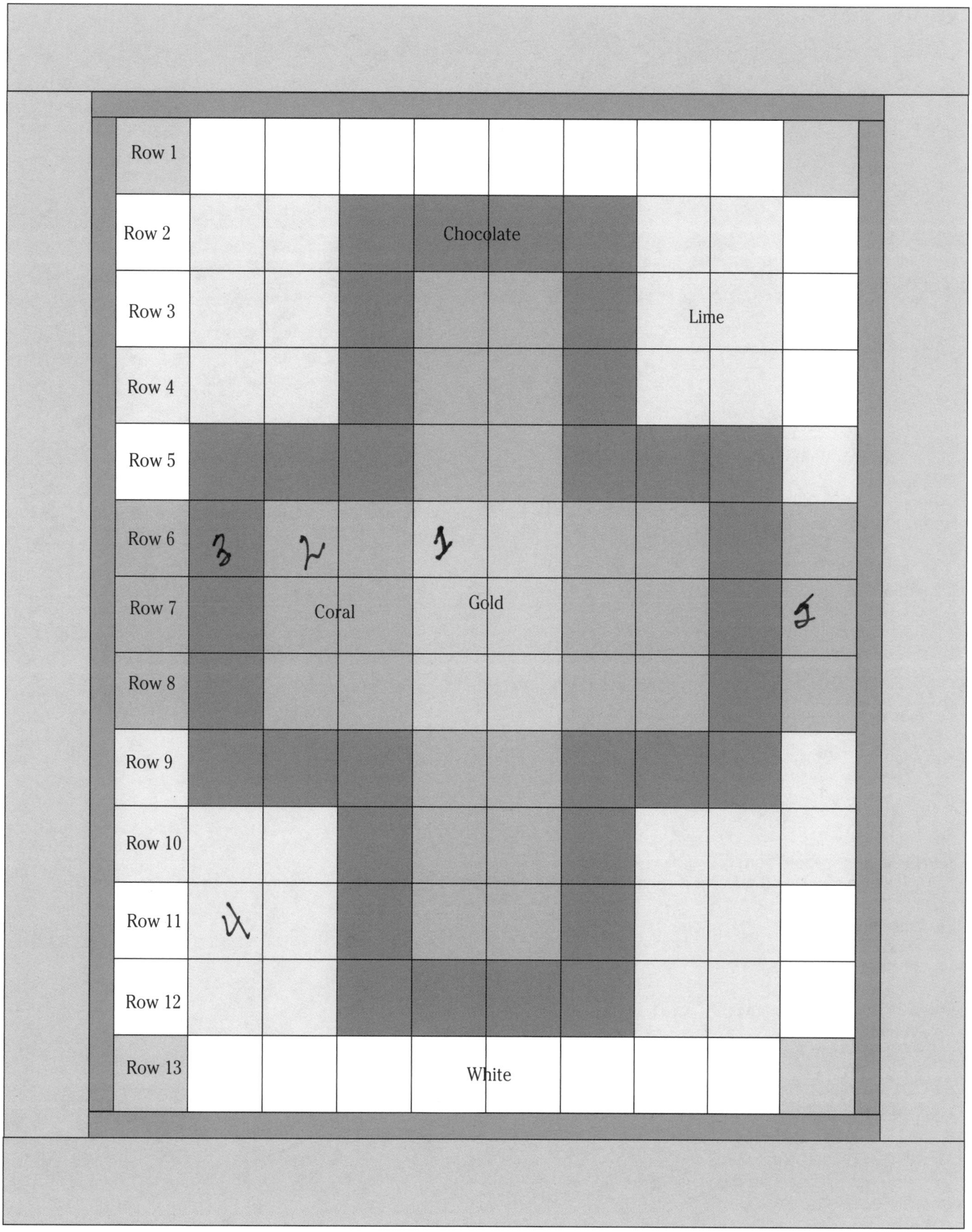

Row 1											
Row 2				Chocolate							
Row 3								Lime			
Row 4											
Row 5											
Row 6	*3*	*2*		*1*							
Row 7		Coral		Gold						*5*	
Row 8											
Row 9											
Row 10											
Row 11	*4*										
Row 12											
Row 13				White							

Retro Blossoms
Quilt Assembly Diagram

photo on page 44

Peaks and Valleys

SIZE: 63¼" x 70"

YARDAGE:
We used *Moda* "Sonnet" by April Cornell
- we purchased 4 'Charm Packs':
(You'll need a total of 148 squares 5" x 5")

27 Green	OR	⅝ yd
34 Brown	OR	¾ yd
36 Orange	OR	¾ yd
36 Aqua	OR	¾ yd
15 Cream	OR	⅓ yd

Stripe Border	Purchase ¼ yd Brown
Outer Border & Binding	Purchase 1½ yds Orange
Backing	Purchase 3¼ yds
Batting	Purchase 69" x 76"

Sewing machine, needle, thread

CUTTING SPLIT TRAPEZOIDS:
You will make these 36 Split-Trapezoids:
6 Aqua-Orange - from Cut A
6 Aqua-Orange - from Cut B
6 Orange-Green - from Cut A
6 Orange-Green - from Cut B
6 Brown-Aqua - from Cut A
6 Brown-Aqua - from Cut B

You need the following squares:
12 Aqua
12 Orange
6 Green
6 Brown
See the Split-Trapezoid Cutting Diagrams A and B.
TIP: To avoid mixing up the pieces, cut one pair at a time.

Cut these following Cutting Diagram A:
3 pairs Aqua-Orange
3 pairs Orange-Green
3 pairs Brown-Aqua
Cut these following Diagram B:
3 pairs Aqua-Orange
3 pairs Orange-Green
3 pairs Brown-Aqua
For each pair, stack 1 square of each color right sides up, NOT
right sides together.

MAKING SPLIT TRAPEZOIDS:
See the Sewing Diagram for Pieced Trapezoids.
Sew pieces together. Press.
Trim to 4¼" x 5".

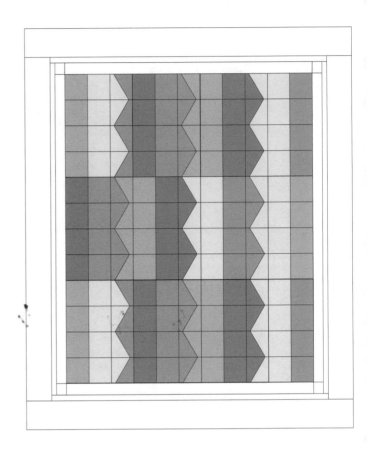

continued on page 32

Split-Trapezoids

IMPORTANT NOTE:
Split-Trapezoids must be cut first
and then sewn.

**Be sure all fabrics are right side up
so the diagonal will be correct.**

Draw a line diagonally as shown on
the diagram, noting whether you
need diagram A or B.

Cut on the line.

Carefully refer to color placement in
Quilt Assembly Diagram.

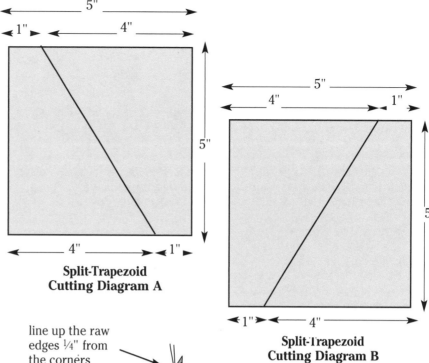

**Split-Trapezoid
Cutting Diagram A**

**Split-Trapezoid
Cutting Diagram B**

Sewing Trapezoid pieces:
With right sides together, carefully line up 2
Split-Trapezoid sections along the diagonal.
Handle these carefully to avoid stretching
this bias edge as you sew.

Line up the corners so the seam will begin at
a raw edge of both fabrics.

Sew ¼" from the diagonal edge of each pair.

Press.

Trim each block to 4¼" x 5".

line up the raw
edges ¼" from
the corners

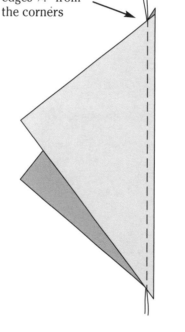

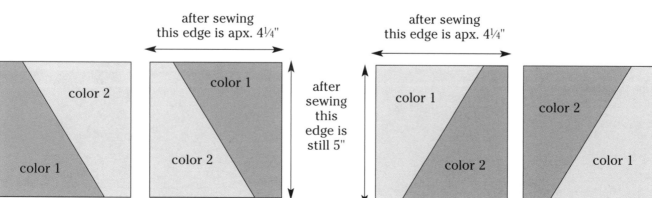

after sewing
this edge is apx. 4¼"

after sewing
this edge is apx. 4¼"

after
sewing
this
edge is
still 5"

color 2

color 1

color 1

color 2

color 1

color 2

color 2

color 1

**After sewing, you will get one of each of these
from a Cut A.**

**After sewing, you will get one of each of these
from a Cut B.**

Finished Split-Trapezoids

continued from page 44

Peaks and Valleys

continued from page 31

BLOCK ASSEMBLY:
Block A: Make 9.
Follow the Assembly Diagram for color placement and direction of the diagonal.
The Split-Trapezoid cuts alternate A-B-A-B in each Block A.

You will make 9 of Block A:
    Sew 4 squares of the same color together end to end for Columns 1. Press.
    Sew 4 squares of the next color together end to end for Column 2. Press.
    Sew 4 Split-Trapezoids together end to end for Column 3. Press.

    Sew the columns together. Press.

Block B: Make 3.
Follow the Quilt Assembly Diagram for color placement.
    Sew 2 columns of 4 blocks each. Press.
    Sew the columns together. Press.

ASSEMBLY:
    Sew 3 of Block A together to form each Column. Press.
    Sew 3 of Block B together to form Column 4. Press.

    Sew the columns together. Press.

BORDERS:
Pieced Border:
For the sides:
    Sew 2 Brown squares, 8 Cream squares and 2 Brown squares
        to make a strip 5" x 54½". Press.
    Cut the strip in half lengthwise to make 2 strips 2½" x 54½".

For top and bottom:
    Sew 7 Cream squares together and trim to 29¾". Press.
    Sew 2 Brown squares to each end. Press.
    Cut the strip in half lengthwise to make 2 strips 2½" x 47¾".
        Cut 1 Green square into 4 squares 2½" x 2½".
        Sew a Green 2½" x 2½" square to each end. Press.

    Sew the side borders to the quilt. Press.
    Sew the top and bottom borders to the quilt. Press.

Stripe Border:
    Cut 2 side strips 1½" x 58½".
    Cut top and bottom strips 1½" x 53¾".
    Sew side borders to the quilt. Press.
    Sew top and bottom borders to the quilt. Press.

Orange Print Border:
    Cut 2 side strips 5½" x 60½".
    Cut top and bottom strips 5½" x 63¾".
    Sew side borders to the quilt. Press.
    Sew top and bottom borders to the quilt. Press.

FINISH:
Quilting: See Basic Quilting Instructions on page 13.
Binding: Cut 2½" strips.
          Sew strips together end to end to make 276".
          Follow Binding Instructions on page 42.

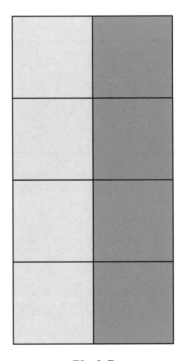

Column 1   Column 2   Column 3

Block A
Make 9
13¼" x 18½"

Block B
Make 3
9½" x 18½"

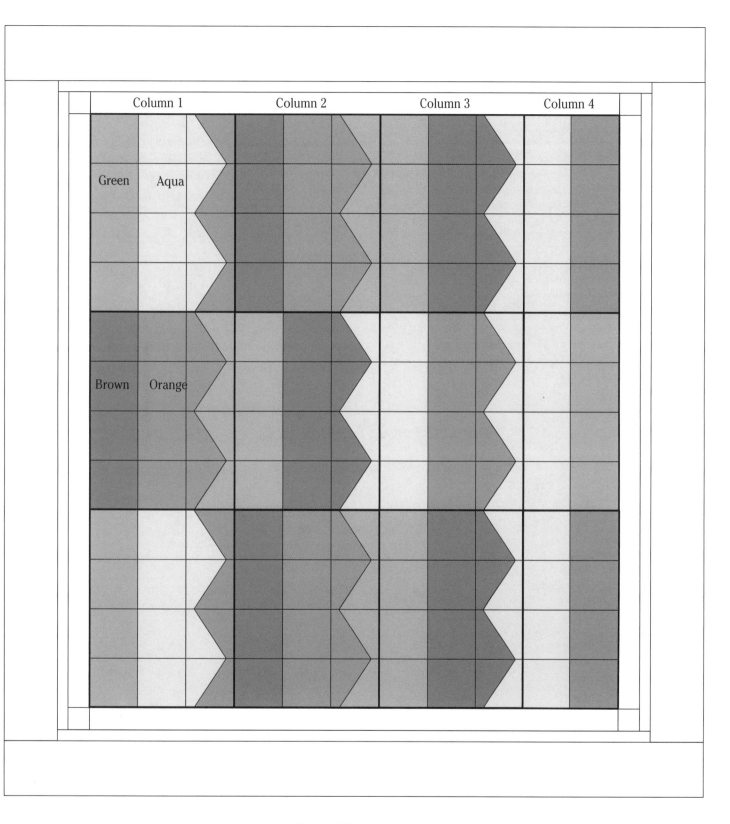

Peaks & Valleys
Quilt Assembly Diagram

Town Square

SIZE: 54½" x 81½"

YARDAGE:
We used *Moda* "Vintage Holiday" by April Cornell
- we purchased 4 'Charm Packs'
(You'll need a total of 160 squares 5" x 5")

48 Green	OR	1 yd
32 Burgundy	OR	⅝ yd
32 Black	OR	⅝ yd
48 Tan	OR	1 yd

Inner Border & Binding   Purchase ⅔ yd Burgundy
Outer Border   Purchase 1 yd Black print
Backing   Purchase 3½ yds
Batting   Purchase 63" x 90"
Sewing machine, needle, thread

CUTTING:
> For rows 1 & 16, cut 4 Green
>   corner blocks 4¼" x 5".
> For rows 2 & 15, cut 4 Burgundy
>   corner blocks 4¼" x 4¼".

40 GREEN-BLACK SPLIT TRAPEZOIDS:
See Instructions for Split Trapezoid on page 31.
Position 20 pairs of Green and Black 5" squares,
>   right sides up,
>   NOT right sides together.
See the Split Trapezoid Cutting Diagrams A and B.
>   Make 10 pairs using Cutting Diagram A and
>   10 pairs using Cutting Diagram B.
Sew pieces together. Press.
>   Trim to 4¼" x 5".

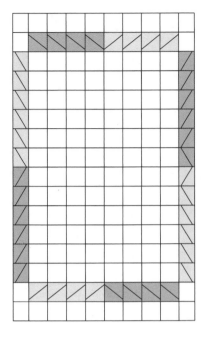

**Positions
for Split
Trapezoids:**

Light shading- A
Dark shading- B

ASSEMBLY:
Follow the Assembly Diagram.
Rows 1 & 16:
>   Begin with a Green 4¼" wide x 5" tall corner block. Sew 8 Green 5" squares together. End with another Green corner block. Press.

Rows 2 & 15:
>   Following the Assembly Diagram, begin and end with a Burgundy 4¼" block. Sew a row of Split Trapezoids, noting the direction of the diagonals and position of the colors. Press.

Rows 3-14:
>   Begin and end each row with a Split Trapezoid, noting the direction of the diagonal and position of the colors. There are eight 5" blocks in each row.
>   Sew all rows. Press.
>   Sew 16 rows together. Press.

BORDERS:
Burgundy Inner Border:
>   Cut 2 side strips 1½" x 71".
>   Cut top and bottom strips 1½" x 46".
>   Sew side borders to the quilt. Press.
>   Sew top and bottom borders to the quilt. Press.

Black Print Outer Border:
>   Cut 2 side strips 5" x 73".
>   Cut top and bottom strips 5" x 55".
>   Sew side borders to the quilt. Press.
>   Sew top and bottom borders to the quilt. Press.

FINISH:
Quilting: See Basic Quilting Instructions on page 13.
Binding: Cut 2½" strips.
>   Sew strips together end to end to make 280".
>   Follow Binding Instructions on page 42.

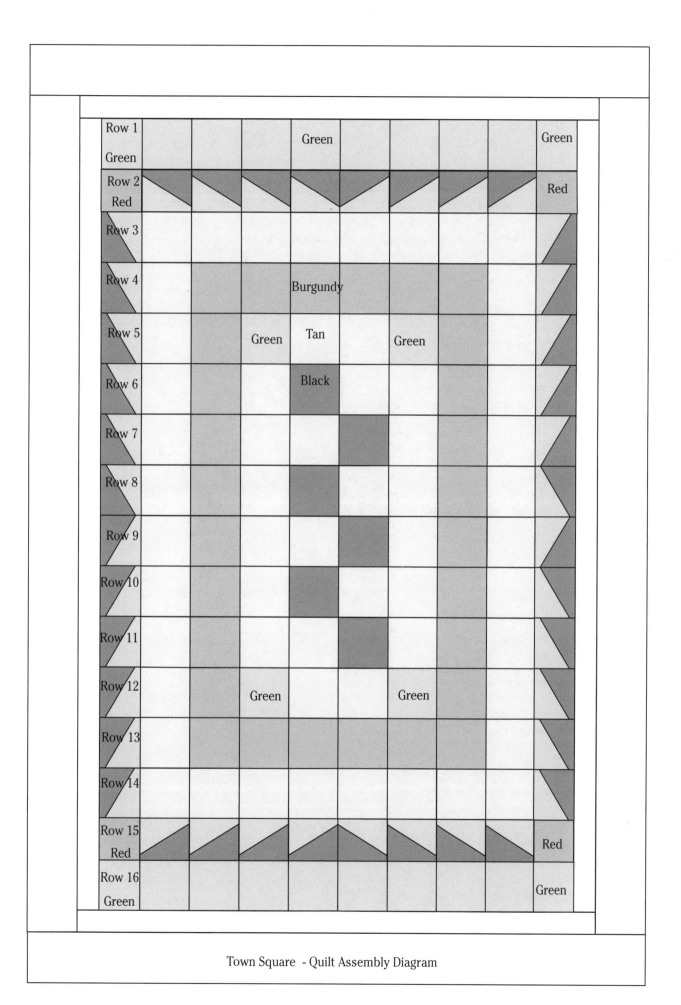

Town Square - Quilt Assembly Diagram

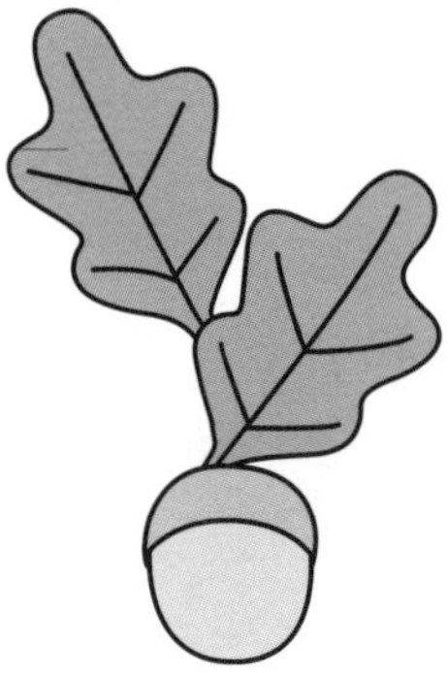

Acorns and Oak Leaves

SIZE: 60½" x 74"

YARDAGE:
We used *Moda* "Oak Leaves and Reel" by
Terry Thompson
- we purchased 4 'Charm Packs':
(You'll need a total of 154 squares 5" x 5")

16 Black to Navy Blue	OR	⅓ yd
8 Brown, Medium to Dark	OR	⅙ yd
16 Burgundy, Medium to Dark	OR	⅓ yd
24 Rust, Medium to Dark	OR	½ yd
20 Green, Medium to Dark	OR	½ yd
28 Tan, Medium to Dark	OR	⅔ yd
42 Tan, Light and leftovers	OR	1 yd

Corner Blocks in Outer Border	Purchase ¼ yd Tan
Outer Border	Purchase 1 yd Burgundy
Binding	Purchase ½ yd Navy Blue
Backing	Purchase 4 yds
Batting	Purchase 69" x 82"

APPLIQUE FABRICS:

Acorns	Purchase ⅛ yd Light Gold or use a 3" x 4" scrap
Acorn Tops	Purchase ⅛ yd Dark Brown or use a 2" x 4" scrap
Leaves	Purchase ⅛ yd Green or use a 10" x 12" scrap

DMC pearl cotton (Dark Brown, Green)
Sewing machine, needle, thread

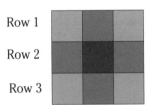

Row 1

Row 2

Row 3

9-PATCH BLOCK ASSEMBLY:
Follow the Assembly Diagram.
This quilt is made of twelve 9-Patch blocks.
For each block, choose 1 Dark, 4 Medium
and 4 Light squares.
    Rows 1 & 3: Sew Light-Medium-Light.
        Press.
    Row 2: Sew Medium-Dark-Medium.
        Press.
Sew the rows together. Press.

QUILT ASSEMBLY:
Sew three 9-Patch blocks together for each
    row. Press.
Make 4 rows.
Sew the rows together. Press

BORDERS:
Inner Border:
For side strips, sew 12 Tan squares together. Press.
For top and bottom strips, sew 9 Tan squares together and
    a Black square on each end. Press.

Sew side borders to the quilt. Press.
Sew the top and bottom borders to the quilt. Press.

Outer Border:
    Cut 2 side strips 6" x 63½".
    Cut top and bottom strips 6" x 50".
    Cut 4 Tan squares 6" x 6" for corner blocks.

    Sew side borders to the quilt. Press.
    Sew a square to each end of the top and bottom strips.
        Press.
    Sew the top and bottom borders to the quilt. Press.

APPLIQUE:
Cut out pieces using the patterns.
Cut the following:
    4 Gold acorns
    4 Brown acorn tops
    8 Green leaves
Position the pieces and applique as desired, see page 11.

EMBROIDERY:
Sew a Running stitch with Green to make the leaf veins.
Sew "X" pattern on the acorn top with Dark Brown.

FINISH:
Quilting: See Basic Quilting Instructions on page 13.
Binding: Cut 7 strips 2½" x 43".
          Sew strips together end to end to make 275".
          Follow Binding Instructions on page 42.

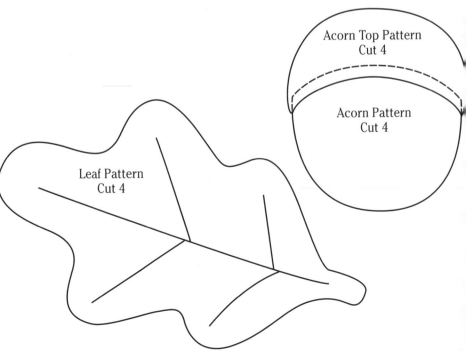

Acorn Top Pattern
Cut 4

Acorn Pattern
Cut 4

Leaf Pattern
Cut 4

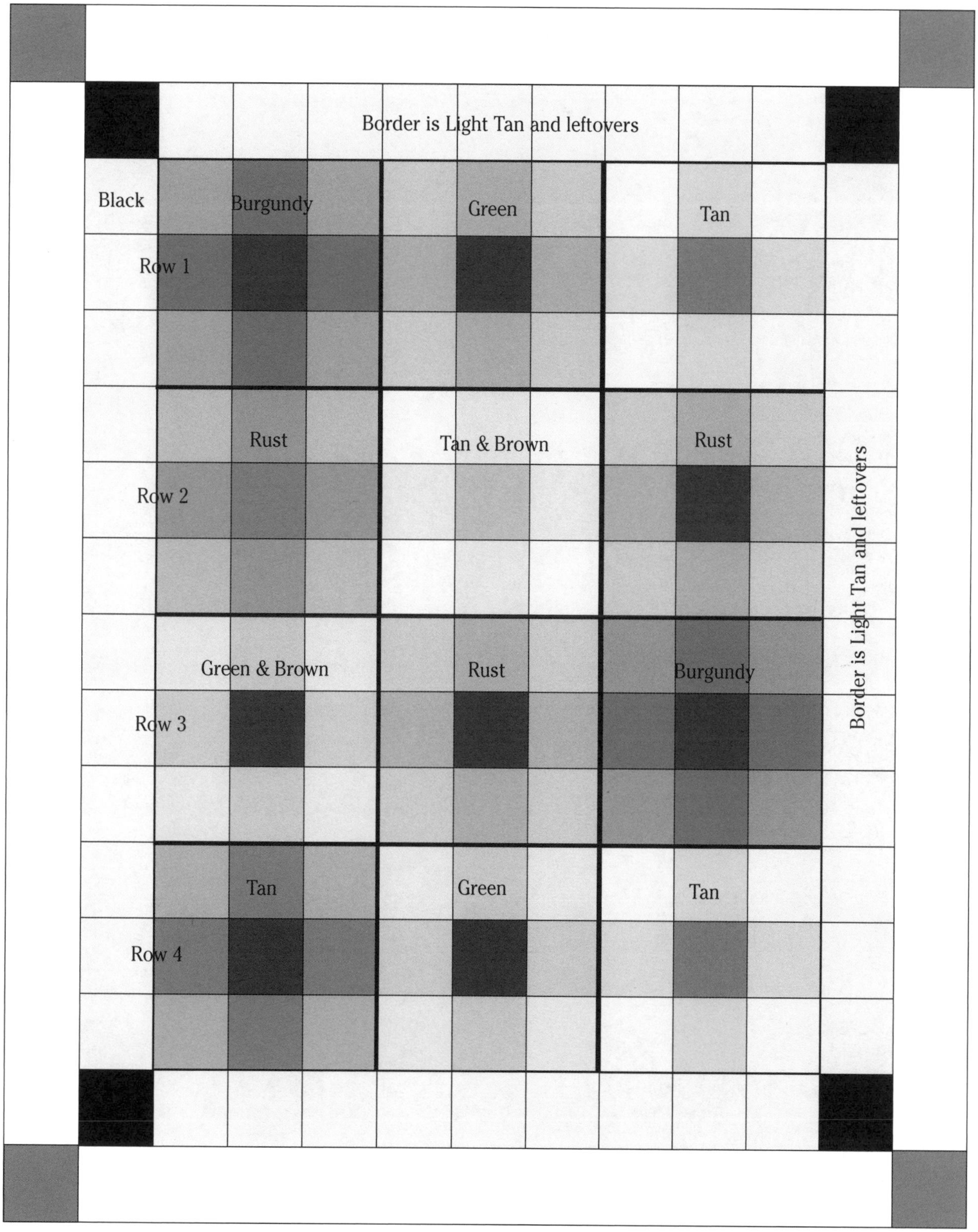

Border is Light Tan and leftovers

Black   Burgundy   Green   Tan

Row 1

Rust   Tan & Brown   Rust

Row 2

Green & Brown   Rust   Burgundy

Row 3

Tan   Green   Tan

Row 4

Border is Light Tan and leftovers

Acorns & Oak Leaves
Quilt Assembly Diagram

photo on page 48

By the Sea

SIZE: 45" x 60½"

YARDAGE:
We used *Moda* "The Hamptons" by Polly Minick and Lauri Simpson
- we purchased 4 'Charm Packs':
(You'll need a total of 135 squares 5" x 5")

20 Red	OR	½ yd
59 White	OR	1⅙ yds
56 Blue	OR	1 yd

Backing   Purchase 2⅛ yds
Binding   Purchase ½ yd White
Batting   Purchase 53" x 69"
Sewing machine, needle, thread

CUTTING:
Cut 20 Red squares in half to make 40 strips 2½" x 5".

ASSEMBLE BLOCKS:
NOTE: Every block A and every block B has 1 White square.
Follow the Assembly Diagram.
Make 8 of Block A. Press.
Make 8 of Block B. Press.
Make 2 of Block C. Press.
Make 2 of Block D. Press.

ASSEMBLY:
Sew the blocks together in columns.
Columns 1 & 3: Sew 4 A Blocks and a C Block. Press.
Columns 2 & 4: Sew a D Block and 4 B Blocks. Press.

Sew the columns together. Press.

BORDER:
Cut 1 White square in half to make 2 strips 2½" x 5".
For each side border, sew 11 White squares and 1 White strip to
    make a strip 5" x 52". Press.
For the top and bottom borders, sew 10 White squares together to
    make a strip 5" x 45½". Press.

Sew the side borders to the quilt. Press.
Sew the top and bottom borders to the quilt. Press.

FINISH:
Quilting: See Basic Quilting Instructions on page 13.
Binding: Cut 2½" strips.
        Sew strips together end to end to make 216".
        Follow Binding Instructions on page 42.

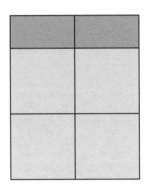

Block A
Columns 1 & 3

Make 8

Block B
Columns 2 & 4

Make 8

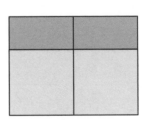

Block C
Located at the
top section
of
Columns 1 & 3

Make 2

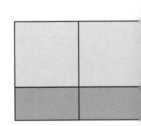

Block D
Located at the
bottom section
of
Columns 2 & 4

Make 2

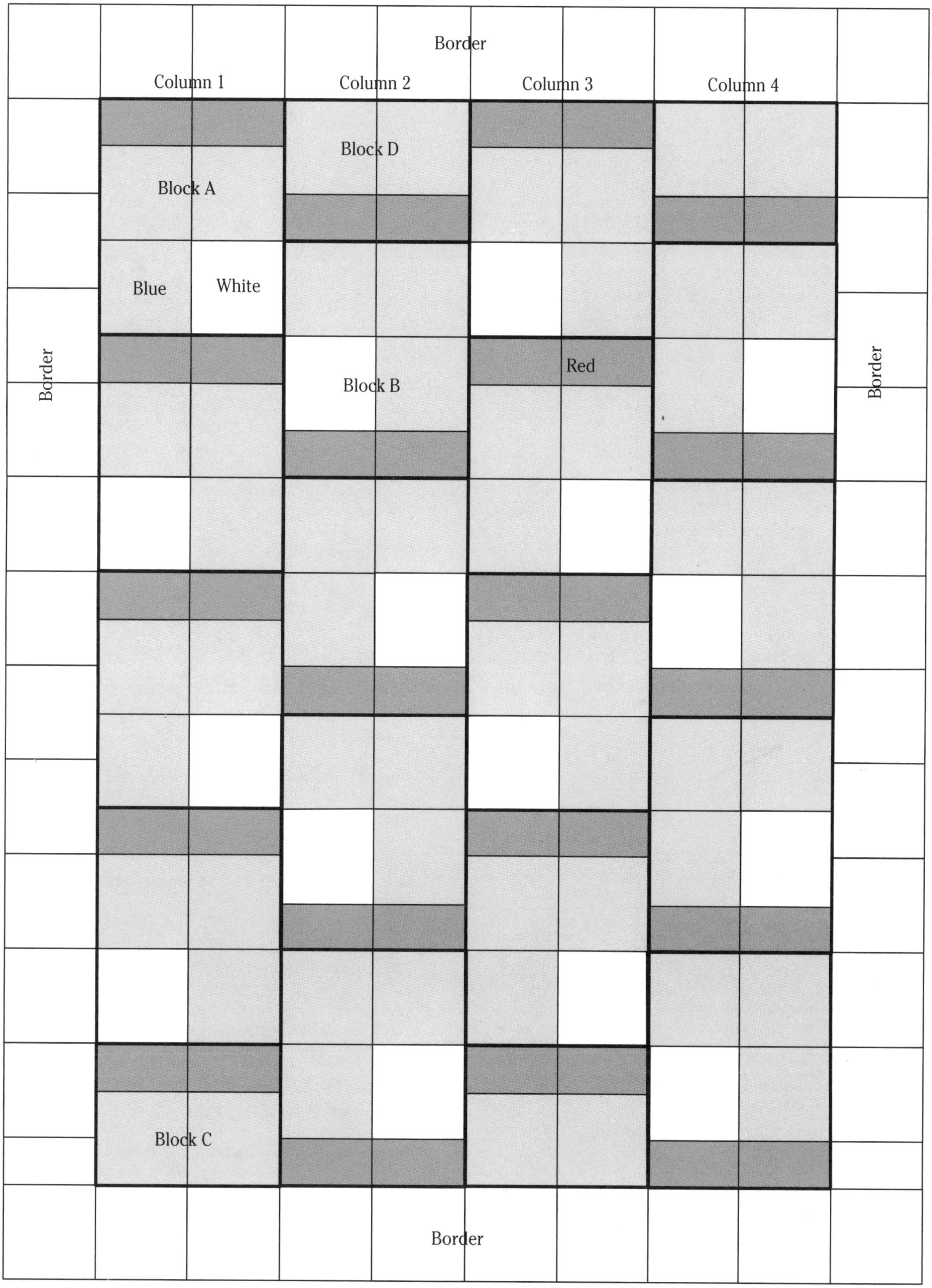

Border

Column 1   Column 2   Column 3   Column 4

Block D

Block A

Blue   White

Border   Border

Red

Block B

Block C

Border

By the Sea
Quilt Assembly Diagram

photo on page 50

Birds in Flight

SIZE: 62" x 66"

YARDAGE:
We used *Moda* "Renewal" by Linda Brannock and Jan Patek
- we purchased 4 'Charm Packs':
(You'll need a total of 140 squares 5" x 5")

25 Black	OR	⅝ yd
21 Red	OR	½ yd
21 Green	OR	½ yd
25 Blue	OR	⅝ yd
28 Brown	OR	⅝ yd
20 Tan	OR	½ yd

Border #4   Purchase ¼ yd Red
Border #5 & Binding   Purchase 1⅝ yds Black
Backing   Purchase 3⅓ yds
Batting   Purchase 70" x 74"
Sewing machine, needle, thread

CUTTING:
For the Block Borders
You will need 40 of block A, 5" x 5":
   4 Black
   11 Green
   12 Blue
   1 Tan
   12 Brown

Cut 4 of block B, 3½" wide x 5" tall:
   2 Green
   2 Brown

Cut 32 of block C, 5" wide x 4¾" tall:
   7 Green
   5 Blue
   6 Tan
   14 Brown

HALF-SQUARE TRIANGLES:
See illustrated instructions on page 14.
Follow the Half-Square Triangle Diagram.
Place a Red square and a Black square right sides together.
Draw a diagonal line with a pencil.
Sew a ¼" seam on each side of the diagonal.
Cut on the diagonal line.
Trim off any dog-ears. Press. Trim squares to 4½" x 4½".

ASSEMBLY:
Follow the Quilt Assembly Diagram.
Noting the position of the colors and direction of the
   diagonal, arrange blocks in 7 rows of 6 blocks per row.
Sew blocks together to form 7 rows. Press.
Sew rows together. Press.

BORDERS
Border #1:
Randomly sew 8 Blue squares together end to end
   to make side borders.
Cut into strips 1½" x 28½" to make 2 side borders. Press.
Cut strips 1½" x 26½" to make the top and bottom. Press.

Sew the side borders to the quilt. Press.
Sew the top and bottom borders to the quilt. Press.

Pieced Border #2:
Cut 13 Tan squares in half to make 26 strips 2½" x 5".
Randomly sew strips together end to end to make
   2 side borders 2½" x 30½".
Randomly sew strips together end to end to make
   top and bottom borders 2½" x 26½".
Sew the side borders to the quilt. Press.

Cut 4 Green corners 2½" x 2½".
Sew a Green square to each end of the top and bottom
   borders to make a strip 2½" x 30½". Press.
Sew the top and bottom borders to the quilt. Press.

Block Border #3:
For each side, sew 2 strips of 8 C blocks in a column to form
   a strip 5" x 34½". Press. For each side, sew 2 strips 5" x
   34½" together side by side to form 9½" x 34½". Press.
Sew sides to the quilt. Press.

For the top and bottom, sew 4 strips of 5 A blocks, 1 B block,
   and 5 A blocks to form strips 5" x 48½". Press.
For top, sew 2 strips together side by side to form a strip
   9½" x 48½". Press.
Repeat for bottom border. Press.
Sew top and bottom borders to the quilt. Press.

Border #4:
Cut 2 side strips 1½" x 52½".
Cut top and bottom strips 1½" x 50½".

Sew the side strips to the quilt. Press.
Sew the top and bottom strips to the quilt. Press.

Border #5:
Cut 2 side strips 6½" x 54½".
Cut top and bottom strips 6½" x 62½".

Sew the side borders to the quilt. Press.
Sew the top and bottom borders to the quilt. Press.

FINISH:
Quilting: See Basic Quilting Instructions on page 13.
Binding: Cut 2½" strips.
Sew strips together end to end to make 264".
Follow Binding Instructions on page 42.

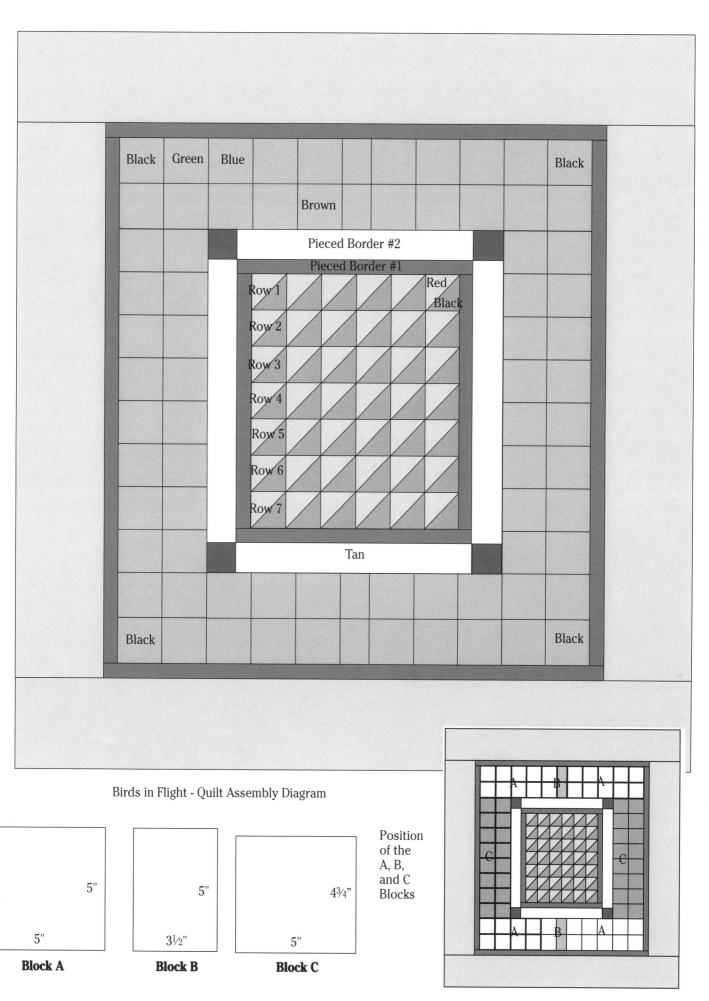

Black Green Blue

Black

Brown

Pieced Border #2

Pieced Border #1

Row 1

Red
Black

Row 2

Row 3

Row 4

Row 5

Row 6

Row 7

Tan

Black

Black

Birds in Flight - Quilt Assembly Diagram

Position
of the
A, B,
and C
Blocks

5"

5"

4¾"

5"

3½"

5"

Block A   **Block B**   **Block C**

A   B   A

C   C

A   B   A

Basic Mitered Binding Instructions

A Perfect Finish:

The binding endures the most stress on a quilt and is usually the first thing to wear out. For this reason, we recommend using a double fold binding.

1. Trim the backing and batting even with the quilt edge.

2. If possible cut strips on the crosswise grain because a little bias in the binding is a Good thing. This is the only place in the quilt where bias is helpful, for it allows the binding to give as it is turned to the back and sewn in place.

3. Strips are usually cut 2½" wide, but check the instructions for your project before cutting.

4. Sew strips end to end to make a long strip sufficient to go all around the quilt plus 4"- 6".

5. With wrong sides together, fold the strip in half lengthwise. Press.

6. Stretch out your hand and place your little finger at the corner of the quilt top. Place the binding where your thumb touches the edge of the quilt. Aligning the edge of the quilt with the raw edges of the binding, pin the binding in place along the first side.

7. Leaving a 2" tail for later use, begin sewing the binding to the quilt with a ¼" seam.

For Mitered Corners:

1. Stop ¼" from the first corner. Leave the needle in the quilt and turn the quilt 90°. Hit the reverse button on your machine and back off the quilt leaving the threads connected.

2. Fold the binding perpendicular to the side you sewed, making a 45° angle. Carefully maintaining the first fold, bring the binding back along the edge to be sewn.

3. Carefully align the edges of the binding with the quilt edge and sew as you did the first side. Repeat this process until you reach the tail left at the beginning. Fold the tail out of the way and sew until you are ¼" from the beginning stitches.

4. Remove the quilt from the machine. Fold the quilt out of the way and match the binding tails together. Carefully sew the binding tails with a ¼" seam. You can do this by hand if you prefer.

Finishing the Binding:

5. Trim the seam to reduce bulk.

6. Finish stitching the binding to the quilt across the join you just sewed.

7. Turn the binding to the back of the quilt. To reduce bulk at the corners, fold the miter in the opposite direction from which it was folded on the front.

8. Hand-sew a Blind stitch on the back of the quilt to secure the binding in place.

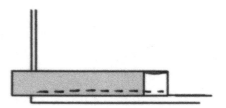

Align the raw edge of the binding with the raw edge of the quilt top. Start about 8" from the corner and go along the first side with a ¼" seam.

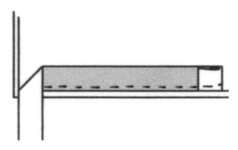

Stop ¼" from the edge. Then stitch a slant to the corner (through both layers of binding)... lift up, then down, as you line up the edge. Fold the binding back.

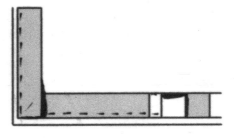

Align the raw edge again. Continue stitching the next side with a ¼" seam as you sew the binding in place.

Retro Blossoms

pieced by Betty Nowlin
quilted by Julie Lawson

For those who loved the avocado greens, mango pinks, and chocolate browns of 1960's décor, this Retro quilt is an "outasight" blast into the past.

This fun and fabulous design is a great beginner project.

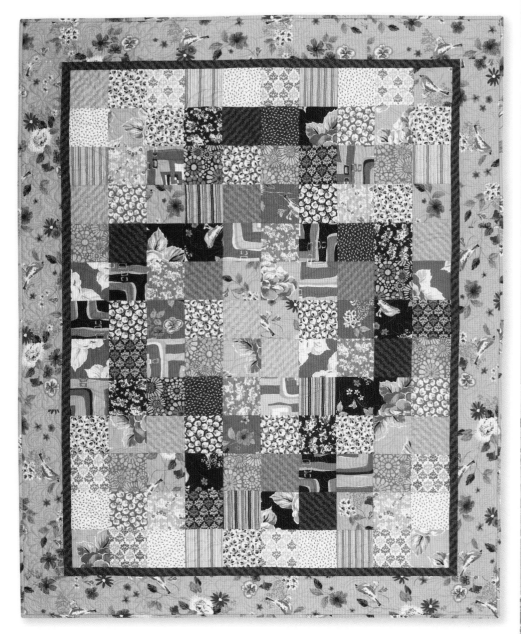

What You'll Need:

SIZE: 57" x 70½"

YARDAGE:

We used *Moda* "Blossom" by Urban Chiks
- we purchased 4 'Charm Packs':
(You'll need a total of 130 squares 5" x 5")

10 Gold	OR	⅓ yd
30 Coral	OR	⅝ yd
30 Lime	OR	⅝ yd
34 Chocolate	OR	¾ yd
26 White	OR	⅝ yd

Inner Border	Purchase ¼ yd Chocolate
Outer Border & Binding	Purchase 1½ yds Floral
Backing	Purchase 3¼ yds
Batting	Purchase 65" x 79"

Sewing machine, needle, thread

continued on page 28

Peaks and Valleys

pieced by
Kayleen Allen
quilted by
Julie Lawson

For a delicious mix of luscious colors that blend readily with your fall decor, try this easy design in orange, teal, brown and green.

Gorgeous prints attract the eye and keep it moving around this fun quilt, inviting your fingers to explore the pretty shapes each square has to offer.

What You'll Need:

SIZE: 63¼" x 70"

YARDAGE:
We used *Moda* "Sonnet" by April Cornell
- we purchased 4 'Charm Packs':
(You'll need a total of 148 squares 5" x 5")

27 Green	OR	⅝ yd
34 Brown	OR	¾ yd
36 Orange	OR	¾ yd
36 Aqua	OR	¾ yd
15 Cream	OR	⅓ yd

Stripe Border	Purchase ¼ yd Brown
Outer Border & Binding	Purchase 1½ yds Orange
Backing	Purchase 3¼ yds
Batting	Purchase 69" x 76"
Sewing machine, needle, thread	

continued on page 30

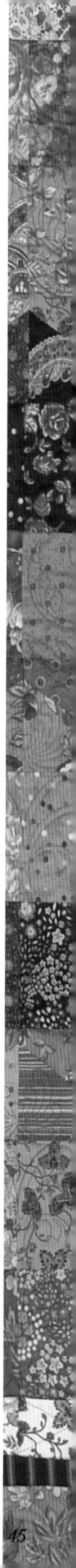

Town Square

*pieced by Betty Nowlin
quilted by Julie Lawson*

Fall and Winter dress the earth in seasonal splendor. Bring the colors of the season to every room with the radiant palette of this gorgeous collection and a fabulous unique design.

What You'll Need:

SIZE: 54½" x 81½"

YARDAGE:
We used *Moda* "Vintage Holiday" by April Cornell
- we purchased 4 'Charm Packs'
(You'll need a total of 160 squares 5" x 5")

48 Green	OR	1 yd
32 Burgundy	OR	⅝ yd
32 Black	OR	⅝ yd
48 Tan	OR	1 yd

Inner Border & Binding	Purchase ⅔ yd Burgundy
Outer Border	Purchase 1 yd Black print
Backing	Purchase 3½ yds
Batting	Purchase 63" x 90"

Sewing machine, needle, thread

continued on page 34

Acorns and Oak Leaves

pieced by Lanelle Herron
applique by Betty Nowlin
quilted by Julie Lawson

The wind feels chill, you see frost on sill, and the morning air tastes crisp and cold. Leaves crunch beneath your shoes as you pick out pumpkins and bedeck your home in the festive colors of Fall.

Get ready for long snuggly nights under comfy quilts and celebrate the season with this family favorite.

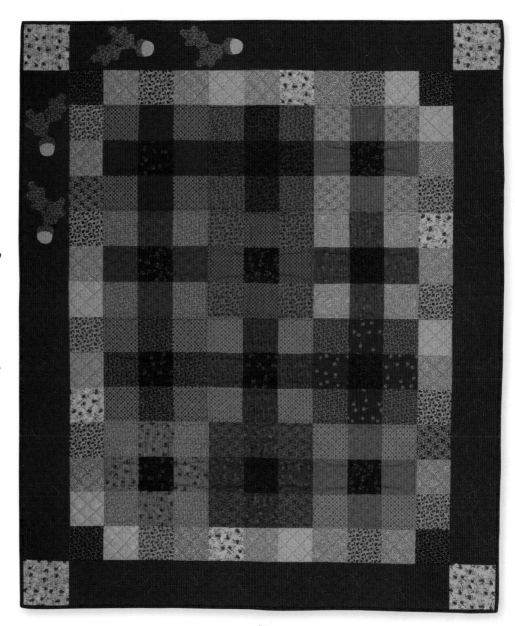

What You'll Need:

SIZE: 60½" x 74"

YARDAGE:
We used *Moda* "Oak Leaves and Reel" by Terry Thompson
we purchased 4 'Charm Packs':
(You'll need a total of 154 squares 5" x 5")

16 Black to Navy Blue	OR	⅓ yd
8 Brown, Medium to Dark	OR	⅙ yd
16 Burgundy, Medium to Dark	OR	⅓ yd
24 Rust, Medium to Dark	OR	½ yd
20 Green, Medium to Dark	OR	½ yd
28 Tan, Medium to Dark	OR	⅔ yd
42 Tan, Light and leftovers	OR	1 yd

Corner Blocks in Border	Purchase ¼ yd Tan
Outer Border	Purchase 1 yd Burgundy
Binding	Purchase ½ yd Navy Blue
Backing	Purchase 4 yds
Batting	Purchase 69" x 82"

APPLIQUE FABRICS:

Acorns	Purchase ⅛ yd Light Gold or use a 3" x 4" scrap
Acorn Tops	Purchase ⅛ yd Dark Brown or use a 2" x 4" scrap
Leaves	Purchase ⅛ yd Green or use a 10" x 12" scrap

DMC pearl cotton (Dark Brown, Green)
sewing machine, needle, thread

continued on page 36

Suzanne McNeill

"I love designing with fabrics. The colors, feel and textures are exciting. Quilts are my favorite!"

Suzanne shares her creativity and enthusiasm in books by Design Originals. Her mission is to publish books that help others learn about the newest techniques, the best projects and popular products.

MANY THANKS to my friends for their cheerful help and wonderful ideas!
Kathy Mason
Patty Williams • Janet Long
David & Donna Thomason
Donna Kinsey for patiently editing the patterns

By the Sea

pieced by
Betty Nowlin
quilted by
Julie Lawson

Breathe in the fragrant salt sea air and dive into fabulous sailboat prints. Patriotic reds, whites, and blues provide a natural setting for this nautical themed quilt.

Make this simple beauty for the sailor in your family or deck out your patio or boathouse for a seaside adventure.

What You'll Need:

SIZE: 45" x 60½"

YARDAGE:
We used *Moda* "The Hamptons"
by Polly Minick and Lauri Simpson
- we purchased 4 'Charm Packs'
(You'll need a total of 135 squares 5" x 5")

20 Red	OR	½ yd
59 White	OR	1⅙ yds
56 Blue	OR	1 yd

Backing   Purchase 2⅛ yds
Binding   Purchase ½ yd White
Batting   Purchase 53" x 69"
Sewing machine, needle, thread

continued on page 38

pieced by
Donna Perrotta
quilted by
Julie Lawson

*Dramatic color pulls
your eye immediately to
the fabulous red and
black center surrounded
by the vibrant colors of
six borders. The fabric
placement creates an
engaging design that
draws the eye around
this masterful quilt.*

Suppliers - Most quilt and fabric
stores carry an excellent assort-
ment of supplies. If you need some
thing special, ask your local store
to contact the following companie

**FABRICS, 'CHARM PACKS',
'JELLY ROLLS','FAT QUARTERS'**
Moda and United Notions,
Dallas, TX, 972-484-8901

QUILTERS
Susan Corbett, 817-361-7762
Julie Lawson, 817-428-5929
Sue Needle, 817-589-1168

What You'll Need:

SIZE: 62" x 66"
YARDAGE:
We used *Moda* "Renewal" by Linda Brannock and Jan
- we purchased 4 'Charm Packs'
(You'll need a total of 140 squares 5" x 5")

25 Black	OR	⅝ yd
21 Red	OR	½ yd
21 Green	OR	½ yd
25 Blue	OR	⅝ yd
28 Brown	OR	⅝ yd
20 Tan	OR	½ yd

Border #4	Purchase ¼ yd Red
Border #5 & Binding	Purchase 1⅝ yds Black
Backing	Purchase 3⅓ yds
Batting	Purchase 70" x 74"
Sewing machine, needle, thread	

continued on page 40